Rosie the Riveter

CORNERSTONES OF FREEDOM

SECOND SERIES

Christine Petersen

Children's Press®
A Division of Scholastic Inc.
New York • Toronto • London • Auckland • Sydney
Mexico City • New Delhi • Hong Kong
Danbury, Connecticut

Photographs © 2005: Corbis Images: 25 (Spencer Beebe), 4, 9,10 top, 11, 13, 14, 15, 16, 18, 20, 24, 26, 32, 34 bottom, 36, 37, 38, 41, 44 (Bettmann), 5, 7 (Hulton-Deutsch Collection), 28 (Edwin Levick/The Mariners' Museum), 19 (Mead Maddick Lownds), 27, 45 right (Minnesota Historical Society), 33 (Genevieve Naylor), 21 (Swim Ink), 29 (John Vachon), 8,12, 34 top; Getty Images/Hulton Archive: 39; Library of Congress: 17 (Edward Gruber), 22, 45 left (Norman Rockwell), cover top, 30, 35; National Archives and Records Administration: cover bottom (J. Howard Miller), 3, 40; U. S. Army via SODA: 10 bottom.

Library of Congress Cataloging-in-Publication Data

Petersen, Christine.

Rosie the Riveter / Christine Petersen.

p. cm. — (Cornerstones of freedom. Second series)

Includes bibliographical references and index.

ISBN 0-516-23634-2

1. Women—Employment—United States—History—20th century—Juvenile literature. 2. World War, 1939–1945—Women—United States—Juvenile literature. 3. World War, 1939–1945—War work—United States—Juvenile literature. I. Title. II. Series.

HD6095.P45 2005

940.53'1—dc22   2004018086

CHILDREN'S PRESS, and CORNERSTONES OF FREEDOM™, and associated logos are trademarks and/or registered trademarks of Scholastic Library Publishing. SCHOLASTIC and associated logos are trademarks and/or registered trademarks of Scholastic Inc.

1 2 3 4 5 6 7 8 9 10 R 14 13 12 11 10 09 08 07 06 05

IN 1943, THE UNITED STATES WAS one of many nations fighting World War II. It was two years after the country had entered the war. Millions of American soldiers were on battlefields in Europe and on the islands of the Pacific Ocean.

In August 1941, the first group of female gas station attendants takes the place of men at a Sunoco station in Pennsylvania.

Newspapers, radio programs, and movies constantly reminded citizens on the home front in the United States that their efforts were also needed if the war was to be won. Americans were asked to **ration,** or use limited amounts of food so that supplies could be sent to soldiers. Everyday materials such as rubber and metal were desperately needed for building weapons. People generously gave up belongings such as cooking pans, dolls, and car tires. These items could be recycled and made into wartime supplies.

As more men went into the military, many jobs were left open. Men who were retired, disabled, or unemployed were asked to step in. Soon women, too, were needed to fill jobs. From 1941 to 1945, nineteen million women worked in factories and businesses, on farms, and in the military. Many of them had never held jobs outside the home before. Now, their efforts made it possible for the United States and its **allies** to win World War II.

"Rosie the Riveter" represents these patriotic women. Rosie was created by the government and the **media.** She was meant to inspire women to continue working for victory. A popular song released in 1943 told Rosie's tale. The song praised Rosie for working to help protect her boyfriend, Charlie, a Marine fighting overseas.

All day long, whether rain or shine,
She's a part of the assembly line,
She's making history working for victory,
Rosie the riveter.

A WOMAN'S PLACE

In the early 1900s, Americans had clear ideas about the roles of men and women. Most people felt that men should take jobs outside the home to support their families. The ideal woman kept a clean and happy home and raised children.

In the early 1900s, most women were expected to stay home and raise children.

★ ★ ★ ★

This attitude became even stronger during the 1930s. At the time, the nation was in a severe economic **depression.** During the Great Depression (1929–1939), one in every five Americans was out of work. Many could not afford homes or food for their families. Some states even passed laws to help keep jobs available for men. For example, in some places it was illegal to hire women.

Yet many American women had no choice but to work. Women of color, recent immigrants, widows, and divorced women had to earn money to support their families. A small number were teachers or nurses. But most women did not have the education or family support needed for these difficult jobs.

Instead, they took what jobs they could get. This usually involved traditional "women's work"—laundry, cleaning, sewing, or cooking. They might also hold positions as waitresses, shop clerks, or typists. Many held jobs in factories, where they canned food, made clothing, or wove fabrics. Countless other women worked alongside men on the farms that fed the nation.

Things were different during wartime. In fact, patriotic women have played an important part in every war. They kept farms and businesses running while men fought during the American Revolution (1775–1783). In the Civil War (1861–1865), women made military uniforms in overcrowded, dangerous factories. In 1915, the government once again asked women to fill the factories. They were needed to make weapons and **ammunition** that would allow American soldiers and their allies to win World War I.

Some women needed an outside job to earn money. This photograph, taken in the 1930s, shows women working in a textile factory.

The Civil War was the first time in American history when women were officially allowed near battlefields, where some served as nurses. At the turn of the twentieth century, the United States Army and Navy accepted female nurses as part of their ranks. Women were even allowed to **enlist** in the armed services during World War I. After World War I ended in 1918, however, most women returned to their lives as housewives and mothers.

The U.S. Navy began enlisting women in 1917, just before the country entered World War I. Female members of the Navy were called Yeomen, or Yeomanettes.

RUMBLINGS OF WAR

For most Americans, World War II began on December 7, 1941. On this day, Japanese fighter planes attacked the U.S. naval base at Pearl Harbor, Hawaii. The attack seemed sudden, but World War II was caused by events that had been unfolding for decades.

World War I ended in 1918 after four years of fierce fighting. The "winners"—the United States, France, Great Britain, Italy, and Japan—divided up land, goods, and money taken from the "losers." Japan was not pleased with the small amount of new territory it received. Its population was growing quickly. The Japanese needed large supplies of natural resources, such as oil and metals, which had to be bought from other countries. In 1931, Japanese troops invaded western China to gain more natural resources and power in Asia.

Trouble also brewed in Europe. After World War I, Germany was forced to sign the Treaty of Versailles. The treaty required Germany to give up control of all its colonies

Government officials from around the world participated in drafting the Treaty of Versailles, at the end of World War I.

A huge crowd of German soldiers stands at attention, listening to a speech by Adolf Hitler in 1936.

Hitler was known as the Führer, or supreme leader, of the German people.

around the world. It also prevented the country from keeping a large army, and it forced the German government to pay a huge amount of money to the winning nations. The German people were left poor and hopeless.

In the election of 1932, Germans showed their frustration by voting for the Nazi Party. The Nazis believed in a strong military. They also believed in the **supremacy** of white Christians over Jews and people of color. As head of the Nazi Party, Adolf Hitler became Germany's leader. He promised to return Germany to its former power. It wasn't long before he had total control over the German government.

In 1938, Hitler took action. He seized control of two of Germany's neighboring nations, Austria and Czechoslovakia. The governments of Great Britain and France promised to protect other nations near Germany if Hitler invaded. On September 1, 1939, German tanks roared into Poland. Two

An armored column of German tanks invades Poland in September 1939.

days later, France and Great Britain declared war against Germany. Another world war was beginning.

TAKING SIDES

In 1939, Italy joined forces with Germany. The following year the two nations attacked France, forcing its surrender. Hitler then turned his attention toward Great Britain. Throughout the autumn, winter, and spring of 1940 to 1941, his army launched surprise attacks on British cities. More than sixty thousand people were killed.

To terrorize Great Britain, Hitler ordered the bombing of London and other cities. Here, firefighters try to put out fires resulting from a recent attack.

Until 1940, most Americans preferred to stay **neutral,** taking no sides in the war. Opinions started to change as it became clear that Great Britain was in trouble. On December 29, 1940, President Franklin D. Roosevelt made a radio announcement to the American public. He said that the United States would provide military equipment to support Britain in the war. Britain was the last free nation separating Europe (now controlled largely by Germany) from the United States. If Britain fell to the Nazis, the United States would be forced to fight alone.

In truth, the United States was not prepared to go to war. World War I had been called "the war to end all wars,"

✳ ✳ ✳ ✳

because people around the world believed that such a terrible event could never happen again. After it was over, the U.S. government allowed the military to become very small. In 1940, Congress approved a military **draft** in case the United States had to enter this new world war. This meant that men were required to sign up for military service.

Richard Ambre of Aurora, Illinois, was one of many American men who left their families to join the Naval Reserves and other branches of the armed forces in 1941.

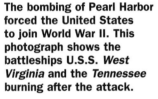

★ ★ ★ ★

Roosevelt also called for the production of large numbers of airplanes, tanks, warships, and other **ordnance.** Factories across America began operating around the clock. Thousands of men—and some women—found work in the busy factories.

Meanwhile, Japan continued its invasion of China. Roosevelt asked the Japanese government to stop, but it refused. He decided it was necessary to send troops to the Philippine Islands, south of Japan in the Pacific Ocean. He hoped to prevent the Japanese from capturing more land.

When Roosevelt cut off Japan's supply of oil and other goods, its leaders grew angry. It wasn't long before Japan

The bombing of Pearl Harbor forced the United States to join World War II. This photograph shows the battleships U.S.S. *West Virginia* and the *Tennessee* burning after the attack.

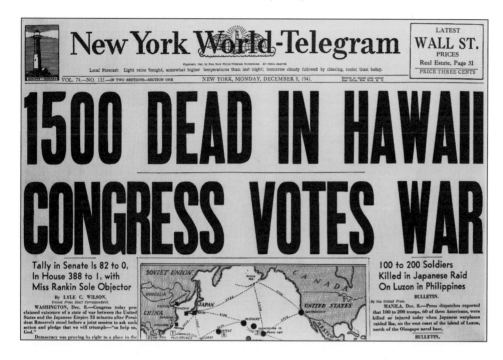

began to plot an attack on the United States. A dozen Japanese warships were sent south toward the Hawaiian Islands. On the morning of December 7, 1941, more than 350 Japanese fighter planes swooped down on the U.S. naval base at Pearl Harbor, on the Hawaiian island of Oahu. The attack took the base by surprise.

Before the Americans could respond, the Japanese dropped hundreds of bombs on the fleet of ships docked in the harbor. Twenty-one ships were sunk or damaged. More than 2,400 American servicemen were killed. President Roosevelt and Congress immediately declared war on Japan.

The United States joined forces with the Allies. This group of nations included France, the Soviet Union, China, Great Britain, Canada, Australia, and New Zealand. They

DEFENSE FACTORIES

In 1941, hundreds of factories manufactured cars, household appliances, cameras, and other common items. But when the United States entered World War II, war materials became more important. Soldiers desperately needed gas masks, machine guns, parachutes, and tanks to fight the enemy. For this reason, many businesses switched to producing ordnance. These were known as "**defense** factories."

Men in Boston, Massachusetts, wait in line to enlist in the Navy following the Pearl Harbor attack.

fought against Germany, Italy, and Japan, which were called the Axis powers. For almost four years, war would be fought on every continent except Antarctica and in every ocean. Tens of millions of people would die in this struggle for freedom. The world would be changed forever.

PRODUCTION SOLDIERS

Americans who worked in the wartime factories were often called production soldiers. These workers battled to produce enough military ordnance so that the Allies could win the war.

The first defense-factory jobs went to men who had not yet been drafted. After Pearl Harbor, young men were being sent to war in ever-increasing numbers. Men who were too old for military service or whose health kept them from fighting took the open jobs. But there simply were not enough men to do the job.

Factories were desperate for workers. Many, however, refused to hire women or people of color. Almost 750,000 women applied for jobs right after the bombing of Pearl Harbor. Fewer than 100,000 were hired. Most men believed that women were not strong enough to work with heavy machinery and were too nervous to work in the noisy, busy factories.

After U.S. entry into the war, many factories began producing ordnance, or war supplies. This photograph shows a man making airplane engines in 1942.

The government's War Department tried to ease employers' concerns. It argued that women would work hard to bring

A woman inspects machine-gun bullets in a factory in Bridgeport, Connecticut. A picture of her husband, stationed overseas, is in the background.

their husbands, sons, and brothers home safely and quickly. Special programs trained men to work with women. Factories were rebuilt so that even the smallest women could run the machinery. Jobs were broken into smaller parts that could be learned quickly. Courses were offered to teach women skilled trades such as welding and machinery repair.

＊ ＊ ＊ ＊

Slowly, defense factories and other businesses began hiring women. Women ordnance workers (nicknamed WOWs) surprised employers with their enthusiasm and skill. But the supply of new WOWs dried up by the summer of 1943. It seemed that every woman who wanted to work had already been hired.

The government anxiously began considering how to find more workers. Officials soon realized that there was one large group of women who had not yet answered the call for

Women manufacture airplane parts at North American Aviation in 1942. Thanks in part to these women, North American produced more aircraft during the war years than any other company in the United States.

DRAFTING WOMEN?

As the United States entered World War II, American men were already being drafted. So it wasn't long before members of Congress considered drafting women—to work. Many members of Congress supported such a law. They thought that all citizens should contribute equally in wartime. Thanks to the "Rosie" campaign, such a draft was never needed.

service: housewives. Housewives had children and busy households to fill their time. They also had paychecks from their husbands, who were working or serving as soldiers. As a result, millions of American homemakers neither wanted nor needed to take jobs outside the home.

Without enough people to work in the defense factories, the Allies faced the possibility of losing the war. President Roosevelt decided to take action. He instructed the government to begin a **publicity campaign**. By spreading the word far and wide, Roosevelt hoped that more housewives would become interested in joining the work force.

President Franklin D. Roosevelt knew that the success of the war depended in part on having enough workers in the defense factories.

MEET ROSIE

The government began to flood the nation with **propaganda.** This was information designed to "sell" housewives on the idea of working. Posters declared, "Women in Industry: We Can't Win Without Them" and "This Is Our War Too, Girls!" One poster showed a sad-looking woman holding a letter from her soldier sweetheart. It read, "Longing Won't Bring Him Home Sooner . . . Get a War Job!"

Magazine articles reminded women that working was their patriotic duty. Short films played in movie theaters tried to convince women that factory work was not so different from housework. Cutting metal airplane parts was compared with trimming the fabric for a dress. Putting together airplane parts was said to be as easy as needlepoint.

This *Women in the War* poster was created in 1942.

Words were not enough, however. American women needed a role model. One poster released by the Westinghouse Corporation caught the nation's attention. It showed a pretty WOW dressed in a pair of blue denim workman's

This picture of "Rosie" appeared on the cover of the *Saturday Evening Post* in May 1943. It reminded all Americans—not just women—of the need for them to do their part to support the war effort.

* * * *

coveralls. A red-and-white bandanna was wrapped around her head, and her lips were painted red. The look on her face was serious. Over her head ran the words "We Can Do It!" This image appealed to many Americans.

Before long, America had another WOW to admire. The May 29, 1943, cover of *The Saturday Evening Post* pictured a woman with bulging muscles and a dirty face. She wore overalls, and goggles and a welding mask sat atop her head. Her elbow rested on a lunchbox with "Rosie" painted on the side. A huge **rivet** gun (used to bolt together airplane parts) sat on Rosie's lap. The colors of the American flag filled the background. This image of Rosie, painted by the famous artist Norman Rockwell, made it clear that women could do anything.

DRESSING THE PART

Most men in defense industries had uniforms, but women did not.

Often, WOWs came to work in pants and fitted blouses. They wore small men's work shoes or boots, or women's shoes with short heels.

To keep their hair out of the way, WOWs wrapped their hair inside a bandanna or tucked it into a net cap.

The campaign worked. Before long, the number of working wives doubled. For the first time in history, more than half of all working women were married mothers over the age of thirty-five. By 1945, six million women worked in the war industries. Together they helped build half of the world's defense products.

LIFE IN THE FACTORIES

Almost half of the wartime employees at aircraft companies such as Douglas Aircraft, Radioplane, and Ford were women. The best-known job in these factories was riveting. Riveting involved "shooting" thousands of boltlike rods, or

23

This photograph, taken in 1943, shows women riveters at work.

rivets, into each plane to hold its metal parts together. Women also engineered and built the machines used to plot an airplane's flight path. Others operated cranes, drove trucks, and ran the giant metal presses that stamped out airplane parts. Women helped build almost 275,000 aircraft between 1942 and 1945.

WOWs also worked in the shipping industry. The Kaiser shipyards in Richmond, California, were among the largest in the nation. To build its ships, Kaiser used assembly lines. Assembly lines consisted of long rows of workers. Each worker did one small task over and over again on different pieces of equipment. This system allowed as many as four huge ships to come out of the Richmond shipyards each week.

During the war, women stepped in and filled roles that no one had believed they were capable of, including the women themselves. But war work was far less exciting than the ads had suggested. Workers often put in long hours, usually with only one day off each week. Vacations were rarely allowed. Many workers were forced to take night shifts because the factories ran around the clock. In addition,

A group of women welders posed for a picture at Ingalls Shipbuilding Corporation in Mississippi in 1943.

WOWs often worked in dark, dirty, and cramped conditions such as the hold of a ship or the narrow body of an aircraft.

The work itself was sometimes dangerous. Women in ammunition factories packaged gunpowder and built bombs and bullets. Some of these jobs were so risky that women worked alone in tiny booths. That way, if they made a mistake the resulting explosion would be contained to a small area. They also built and tested rifles and machine guns. Injuries were common, and a few WOWs lost their lives in factory accidents.

To make matters worse, companies usually paid male employees more than female workers. For example, male factory workers at the Redstone **Arsenal** in Alabama

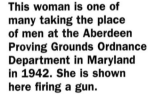

This woman is one of many taking the place of men at the Aberdeen Proving Grounds Ordnance Department in Maryland in 1942. She is shown here firing a gun.

* * * *

"I've found the job where I fit best!"

FIND YOUR WAR JOB
In Industry – Agriculture – Business

This poster urges women to find a "war job."

earned an average of thirty dollars during a six-day work-week. Women doing the same jobs made barely twenty-two dollars a week.

Still, WOWs were glad to do their part for the war effort. Every American soldier's life depended on the ordnance built. Women ordnance workers took their responsibility seriously. They trusted that their work would help win the war—and it did.

WORKING OUTSIDE THE FACTORIES

Thirteen million women held jobs other than ordnance work during World War II. Their work was not as celebrated as

★ ★ ★ ★

An American Red Cross unit on its way to Europe in 1944.

WAR BONDS

The U.S. government asked Americans to help pay for the war by purchasing war bonds. Each bond cost $18.75 and could be redeemed after ten years for $25.

that of the WOWs, but it was just as important. In the absence of men, women ran shops and drove ambulances. They worked as lumberjacks and miners, fought fires, and moved baggage on trains. Thousands also joined the "land army." They worked on farms to make sure that milk, meat, grains, fruits, and vegetables were available to Americans.

Some women could not take paid jobs. Instead, they did important volunteer work. They grew "victory gardens" that provided fresh food for their communities. Many sold war bonds that helped pay for the war. About six thousand women volunteered for the Civil Air Patrol. These women kept a nightly lookout for enemy aircraft along U.S. shorelines.

The most successful volunteer organization was the American Red Cross (ARC). ARC workers staffed the blood banks and offered first aid. They also prepared bandages for hospitals overseas and helped the families of soldiers. Some even risked their lives by going to work directly with the soldiers in Europe and the Pacific.

MINORITIES STRUGGLE FOR WORK

The United States may have been fighting for freedom in World War II, but it had not yet learned to treat all of its citizens equally. Most white people didn't want to work with or live near people of African, Latin American, Asian, or Native American descent. Men in these groups were required to fight for their country. But back at home, laws still allowed employers to avoid hiring nonwhites.

In 1941, African Americans threatened to hold a huge protest march in Washington, D.C., if these laws were not changed. In response, President Roosevelt created the

Many African Americans protested unfair labor laws at home in the United States.

Fair Employment Practices Committee. This group of people would help enforce the hiring of African Americans, Latinos, and Asians.

African American educator Mary McLeod Bethune was among those working for equality. She tried to get black women admitted to the Department of Labor's training pro-

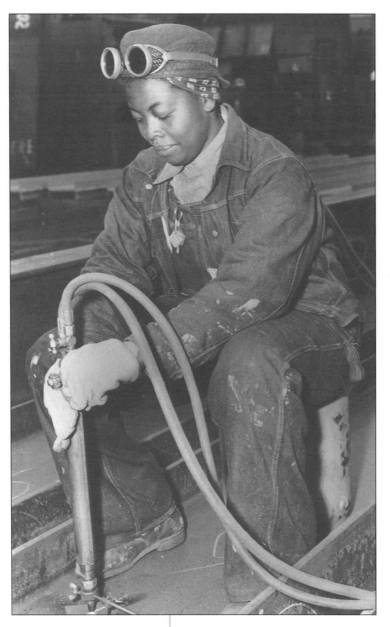

An African American woman helps build the SS *George Washington Carver* at Kaiser shipyards. In 1943, about 1,000 black women worked at the shipyards.

grams for WOWs. Throughout the war, she and other African Americans called for a "double victory." They wanted not only to win the fight against our enemies overseas but also to stop people of color from being treated unfairly at home.

As a result of Bethune's efforts, some black women were able to leave jobs as domestic servants and field workers. They could earn a little more money doing war work. They still weren't treated the same as their white coworkers, however. In factories, African American women were often assigned to cleanup crews. Or, they were given the most dangerous jobs, such as building ammunition or unloading heavy boxes of freight. Blacks often were placed on the night shift to separate them from white workers.

These problems did not stop African Americans. More than 600,000 black women contributed to the war effort. They worked both to support their families and to bring their men home safely.

HARDSHIPS ON
THE HOME FRONT

The war was a difficult time for everyone. Even simple chores such as banking or grocery shopping became a problem for working mothers. Most of these businesses closed before the day shift ended.

Some shops and businesses helped out by staying open one or two evenings each week. Department stores sometimes brought clothing samples to factories for women to look at on their lunch breaks. In some cases, volunteers came to the factories and took grocery orders. They would then deliver the food to workers at the end of their shifts.

WORKING MOTHERS

A working mother's day was far from over when she returned home in the evening. Working moms had to prepare meals, clean the house, go shopping, and do laundry. And remember—most women didn't have dishwashers and washing machines to make these tasks easier!

Another challenge was the shortage of items that people used in their daily lives. The war industries needed huge amounts of gasoline, rubber, metals, and even sugar and cooking fat. Every American had to use less.

To enforce these limits, the government began to print ration books. These books contained coupons allowing each person certain amounts of sugar, milk, meat, butter, and other items for each month. Gasoline was rationed as well.

Once they used up their coupons, people had to do without until the next month. Most citizens took pride in their ability to survive on less. They learned to get around by walking, bicycling, sharing rides, or taking public transportation.

Child care was another difficulty. A few large factories opened centers to care for employees' young children. But

Above, a woman uses ration coupons to buy food. Ration coupons for gasoline are shown at right. Most people were only allowed 3 to 4 gallons (11–15 liters) of gas per week.

most employers considered child care a minor problem. They figured that women would go back to being house-wives after the war. The problem would then be over.

In the meantime, working mothers left their children with family members or neighbors. Older children might care for younger siblings, while children who didn't have siblings often stayed home alone after school. Some women cooperated with friends. By working different shifts, they could take care of each other's children.

Of all the home-front concerns, housing may have been the most serious. More than twenty-five million people **migrated** from farms and small towns to find work at defense factories in larger towns and cities. There was no way to meet the demand for housing. Married women workers might be lucky enough to own homes already, but single women usually had to rent. There were so few rooms available that women often slept two to a bed. They then turned their rooms over to another pair of girls when they went to work. Migrant families had it even harder. They sometimes had to sleep in tents or out in the open.

Towns found it hard to provide enough clean water, health care, or room in the schools for their ever-growing popula-

Children walk down a hall-way in their pajamas at the Henry Kaiser Portland Ship-yard's daycare center. This was one of the first daycare centers for children whose mothers worked in military manufacturing.

33

* ★ ★ ★ ★

During the war, trailers such as these served as housing for many factory workers.

Representative Edith Nourse Rogers introduced a bill to Congress that would result in the creation of the Women's Army Corps (WAC).

tions. In some places, the government was forced to build housing for single workers or put in rows of small trailers for families.

WOMEN IN THE RANKS

A year before the United States entered the war, Massachusetts congresswoman Edith Nourse Rogers knew there would be a need for women in the U.S. military. In May 1941, Rogers introduced a bill to Congress to address this need. The bill called for the creation of a women's branch in the Army. This would be in addition to the official nursing units of the Army and the Navy, which were made up almost entirely of women. Rogers reminded Congress that almost 13,000 women had served in the military during World War I. But many people did not take her plan seriously.

Pearl Harbor changed everything. Six months after the United States entered World War II, President Roosevelt signed Representative Rogers's bill into law. The Women's Army Corps (WAC) became a reality. The Navy soon followed with its WAVES (Women Accepted for Voluntary Emergency Service) program. The Coast Guard and the Marines also opened their ranks to women in 1942. More than 300,000 women enlisted in the new wartime military services. Another 74,000 women served in the Army and Navy nurse corps during World War II.

ENLIST IN THE WAVES

U.S. NAVY

RELEASE A MAN TO FIGHT AT SEA

Apply to your nearest
NAVY RECRUITING STATION OR OFFICE OF NAVAL OFFICER PROCUREMENT

Posters such as this one recruited women to enlist in WAVES. This naval organization was created in 1942 so that more men would be free to fight at sea.

More than 150,000 American women served in the WAC during World War II.

Women who enlisted in the WAC, the WAVES, the Marines, and the Coast Guard went through boot camp, a military training program. Their program was similar to that of male soldiers. The difference was that women were not trained in the use of weapons. The main role of military women was not to go to war. It was to take over jobs on the home front, freeing men to fight. Women performed at least 250 types of jobs for the military. These included typists, radio operators, and translators.

Some women did go overseas during the war. Many members of the Army and Navy nurse corps were stationed at hospitals near battlefields. They often performed their duties under life-threatening conditions. Some were even held as prisoners of war along with American soldiers.

Members of the Army's all-black 6888th Central Postal Directory Battalion also served overseas. They were stationed in England and France beginning in early 1945. The women of the 6888th were responsible for getting mail to and from soldiers across Europe. Finally, about 17,000 WACs were sent overseas as well. They served in countries in Europe, Asia, Africa, and other parts of the world.

Hundreds of female pilots were also eager to join the military. As the war progressed, the Army's Air Force

As part of their training to serve overseas, these U.S. Army nurses carry heavy combat packs on a hike through the jungle.

division finally decided to hire women. Two experienced pilots were Jacqueline Cochran and Nancy Love Harkness. Each was put in charge of separate teams, and a training program was started.

Taken in 1943, this photograph shows two women, Elizabeth McKinley and Elenor Boysen, who have just completed flight training. They would soon be serving as part of the U.S. Air Force.

More than 25,000 women applied to become WASPs, or Women's Airforce Service Pilots. Of that number, almost 1,100 women completed the training. They flew more than 60 million miles (96.5 million kilometers) by the end of the war. WASPs delivered people and supplies to military bases across the United States. They tested aircraft and worked with engineers to improve designs. Their most important job was to deliver newly built airplanes from factories to bases. From there the airplanes would be shipped overseas.

WINNING THE WAR

Throughout 1944 and 1945, the Allies won one victory after another. The successful D-Day invasion of Normandy, France, took place on June 6, 1944. Seven thousand ships holding almost 200,000 Allied soldiers landed on Normandy's beaches that morning. They fought their way inland against German troops. By nightfall the battle was won. It gave Allied troops hope that the war would soon end.

U.S. troops hold a captured Nazi flag in France, after the success of D-Day.

During the next few months, the Allies continued to push past German forces in France. The Battle of the Bulge, which began on December 16, 1944, was Hitler's last attempt to defeat the Allies. He lost, and the Allies entered Germany in April 1945. Sensing defeat, Hitler committed suicide. Germany surrendered in early May.

The war was not going as well for the Allies in the Pacific. Japan continued to fight despite the defeat of the other Axis powers. It was expected that troops would soon have to invade Japan. President Harry Truman (who took over after Roosevelt's death in April 1945) knew that up to one million soldiers might be killed in such an invasion. To prevent this, he agreed to take a drastic step.

On August 6, 1945, a bomber pilot flew his plane over the Japanese city of Hiroshima. He dropped Little Boy,

A "mushroom" cloud of radioactive vapor rose over Nagasaki, Japan, after the atomic bomb was dropped. Sixty thousand men, women, and children died within seconds.

★ ★ ★ ★

a 9,000-pound (4,082-kilogram) atomic bomb. It was the deadliest weapon ever built. The bomb exploded with a blinding flash and a wave of energy that flattened everything in its path. Within seconds 60,000 Japanese men, women, and children were dead. In the days (and years) that followed, tens of thousands more died of poisoning from the chemicals released by the bomb. On August 9, a second atomic bomb was dropped on Nagasaki. Five days later, Japan's emperor surrendered.

With the war over, the U.S. government ended its production of ordnance. Soon, a new propaganda campaign began. This one encouraged women to quit their jobs. Soldiers who were coming home would need the work. Women were expected to return to their former roles as housewives.

Many women accepted this change. Some were even relieved. Yet others were saddened by the loss of jobs they had worked so hard to earn. Women who had always worked still needed to do so. Some had lost their husbands in the war and had to support their families. For them, the end of the war

Many women remained in the workforce in the 1950s, trying out new kinds of jobs. Here, two women work as computer operators in 1955.

HONORING ROSIES

To honor the important work of women in World War II, a national park was established in October 2000. The Rosie the Riveter/World War II Home Front National Historical Park is located in Richmond, California. It allows visitors to observe the assembly lines, housing, and other buildings used by 90,000 Kaiser shipyard workers during the war. The park is also home to the S.S. *Red Oak Victory*. It is one of the last remaining Victory-class cargo ships built by Rosies in Richmond during the war.

meant that jobs were harder to find and offered lower pay. War work had shown other American women how much they could accomplish, and they were hesitant to go back to "women's work." Polls showed that as many as three-quarters of all WOWs would have liked to keep their jobs.

For a while, women shifted their attention to rebuilding their homes and families. But small changes were underway. The number of working women remained high—in 1950 more than one-third of American women held jobs. Over the following decades, women began to try out new kinds of jobs and take on new levels of independence. Thanks to the pioneering women of World War II, twenty-first-century women really can do it all.

Glossary

allies—a group of people or nations joined together to accomplish a shared goal

ammunition—bullets, missiles, bombs, and other explosive materials used as weapons

arsenal—a collection of military equipment such as guns and ammunition, or a factory that manufactures such weapons

defense—a form of protection, such as a country's military forces

depression—a time when unemployment and poverty are high

draft—a legal order requiring men to sign up for military service in wartime

enlist—to join the armed services

media—system of communication, such as newspapers, television, etc.

migrate—to move from one place to another

neutral—taking no sides in a war or a disagreement

ordnance—military supplies such as airplanes, guns, and tanks

propaganda—information intended to make people believe a particular idea or cause

publicity campaign—a widespread effort to bring attention to an event, a person, or an idea

ration—to limit the amount of something a person can have

redeem—to exchange a bond or a coupon for cash or goods

rivet—a short metal rod used to attach airplane parts together

supremacy—a belief that one person or group is better than another

Timeline: Rosie the

SEPTEMBER 1
Germany invades Poland

OCTOBER
The first peacetime military draft begins

DECEMBER
President Roosevelt gives a radio talk announcing that the U.S. will provide war supplies to Great Britain

DECEMBER
Japanese planes bomb Pearl Harbor; the U.S. enters World War II on the side of the Allies

Riveter

1942

The Women's Army Corps is established; the Navy, the Marine Corps, and the Coast Guard begin enlisting women

1943

The "Rosie" propaganda campaign begins to attract more women into war jobs; the Women's Airforce Service Pilots (WASP) program is formed

"I've found the job where I fit best!"

FIND YOUR WAR JOB
In Industry – Agriculture – Business

THE SATURDAY EVENING
POST
BEGINNING—A NEW KELLAND SERIAL
Heart on Her Sleeve
EDGAR SNOW REPORTS ON GERMAN ATROCITIES

1944

U.S. government ends the recruitment of women workers

1945

MAY
Germany surrenders unconditionally

AUGUST
U.S. drops atomic bombs on the Japanese cities of Hiroshima and Nagasaki; Japan surrenders, and World War II officially ends

To Find Out More

BOOKS

Colman, Peggy. *Rosie the Riveter: Working Women on the Home Front in World War II.* New York: Crown Publishers Inc., 1995.

Gerdes, Louise I. (ed.). *The 1940s.* San Diego, CA: Greenhaven Press Inc., 2000.

Klam, Julie. *The War at Home.* North Mankato, MN: Smart Apple Media, 2003.

Zeinert, Karen. *Those Incredible Women of World War II.* Brookfield, CT: The Millbrook Press, 1994.

ONLINE SITES

World War II Posters: Women's Roles
http://womenshistory.about.com/library/pic/bl_p_wwii_posters_index.htm

Women Pioneers in American Memory
http://memory.loc.gov/learn/features/women/work.html

Rosie the Riveter/WWII Home Front National Historical Park
http://www.nps.gov/rori/

Rosie the Riveter/World War II Home Front National Park
http://www.rosietheriveter.org

U.S. Army Ordnance Corps. "Rosie the Riveter:
More Than a Poster Girl"
http://www.goordnance.apg.army.mil/rosie.htm

Index

Bold numbers indicate illustrations.

About the Author

Christine Petersen is an educator who lives near Minneapolis, Minnesota. She has also worked as a biologist studying the natural history and behavior of North American bats. When she's not chasing after her young son, Christine enjoys snowshoeing, canoeing, birdwatching, and writing educational books for young people. She is a member of the Society of Children's Book Writers and Illustrators and is the author of more than a dozen books for Children's Press.